Greed & Politics Is Burning Down The Lungs Of The Earth . . .

The Curious Case Of Wildfires In The Amazon Rainforest.

By- M . B . Sattar

<u>*Author's Note*</u>

This Book Is Not To Criticise Anyone Or Distort Anyone's Image. This Book Contains Facts That Are A No Secret To The World. My Aim In Writing This Book Is Not To Get Sensational Reads But My Aim Is To Make People Aware Of The Environmental Disasters That Are Very Harmful To The World.

If You Like This Book, It's A Humble Request To Please Take Some Time And Write Your Precious Review On The Website You Purchased This Book. Your Little Time Taken Would Be Very Inspirational To Write Down Our Next Book On Some Of The Burning Hot Topics Which The World Needs To Know.

Thank You

- M . B . Sattar

Introduction

THE AMAZON RAINFOREST is the largest rainforest in the world. It extends for 3,000 mi (4,828 km) from the Andes mountains to the Atlantic Ocean. The rainforest covers parts of Brazil, Peru, Ecuador, Columbia, Bolivia and Venezuela, encompassing over a billion acres and covering one-third of South America. The 6,500 mi (10,461 km) of the great Amazon River, second only to the Nile River in length, flows throughout the rainforest. Eleven hundred tributaries, some of which are over 1,000 mi (1,609 km) long, feed into the Amazon River.

Since the rainforest is close to the equator, its climate is hot and humid at all times. From 40 to 80 in (100 cm to 200 cm) of rain falls annually in the eastern section of the rainforest, while the western region experiences around 160 in (400 cm) of rain each year. Thunderstorms occur more than 200 days of the year. In sections of the rainforest that are closest to the equator, rain falls almost constantly. Trees within the rainforest are always green, but many shed their leaves in response to biological and climatological changes.

The Amazon Rainforest is considered a resource for the entire world, in part because of the plant life that protects the world's environment from the greenhouse effect. When the rainforest performs its natural function, at last 50 percent of the rain returns to the atmosphere on the leaves of trees through the process of evapotranspiration. This process uses the water loss from the trees in the rainforest to form clouds that make rain in other, more protected parts of the rainforest area.

The rainforest is made up of four layers: the emergent layer, the canopy, the understory, and the forest floor. The emergent layer is located at the top of the trees of the rainforest. This layer is subject to intensive amounts of sunlight, high temperatures, low humidity, and strong winds. The canopy, sometimes called the upper canopy, is made up of the tallest trees in the forest. These trees, which may grow to 200 ft (61 m), protect the land below from harsh sunlight. The middle layer of the rainforest, known as the understory or lower canopy, may be as high as 20 ft (6 m). It is made up of various small trees, vines, and shrubs. The forest floor or the jungle is composed of ground cover such as herbs, mosses, and fungi. The wildlife in this section of the rainforest eats roots, seeds, leaves, fruit, and smaller animals.

Around two-thirds of all animals and plants in the rainforest inhabit the canopy. For instance, in a section of a canopy in the Peruvian rainforest, scientists identified over 50 species of ants, 1,000 species of beetles, some 1,799 arthropod species, and approximately 100,000 species of fauna. Samples taken from canopies in Panama, Brazil, Peru, and Bolivia revealed over 1,500 species of beetles in each canopy. Because the canopy area is not easily accessed and because many insects find shelter underneath the leaves, it is thought that thousands of species may yet be discovered. Some species of wildlife spend their entire lives in the trees of the rainforest.

Poverty, population growth, greed, and short-sightedness have historically been the major threats to the Amazon Rainforest. Construction, which often operates on the principle of "slash and burn," has created a new threat since the middle of the 20th century. For instance, in February 2001, officials in Ecuador contracted with an international consortium to construct the 300-mi (483-km) Oleoducto de Crudos Pesados (Heavy Crude Pipeline) intended to transport crude oil from the rainforest to the Pacific Coast, affecting forests and wildlife and displacing native inhabitants.

RAINFOREST SOILS

Three major soil types have been identified within the Amazon Rainforest. One layer, known as ultisols, is made up of kaolinite clay and minerals that are transported from flooded upper soil levels. This acidic soil, containing aluminium compounds, is not conducive to plant life.

A second layer, called oxisols, which is made up solely of kaolinite clay, is thick and sticky and virtually unusable to plants. Spoldsol soils, which are found in higher lands that are not subject to flooding, tend to be sandy and acidic and are incapable of retaining nutrients. Soils in the rainforest are generally unable to absorb water, further contributing to the difficulties that local farmers face. On the other hand, soils within wetter parts of the rainforest provide an excellent growing area for exotic tropical plants, many of which serve as food for animals in the rainforest.

FAUNA AND FLORA

Around 80 percent of all food eaten by the people of the world today originated in the tropical rainforests, including over 3,000 species of fruit. Edible produce from the Amazon Rainforest include: Brazil nut, cashew, banana, fig, coffee, cocoa, vanilla, passion flower, breadfruit, yucca, avocado, coconut, orange, lemon, grapefruit, guava, pineapple, mango, tomato, corn, tomato, potato, rice, winter squash, yam, black pepper, cayenne pepper, chocolate, soybean, cinnamon, clove, ginger, sugarcane, tumeric, and coffee. Orchid, philodendron, bamboo, mahogany, and rubber fungus are also found in the rainforest.

More animals and plants are found within the Amazon Rainforest than in the rest of the world combined. At least 500 species of mammals, 175 varieties of lizards, 300 species of other reptiles, and innumerable species of tree climbers are among the many animals identified so far. Scientists and environmentalists believe that there are thousands of species of wildlife in the rainforest that have yet to be identified. Some of the animals found in the rainforest include anaconda, ant, anteater, beetle, boa constrictor, pit viper, butterfly, katydid, piranha, capybara, caiman, coatimundi, kinkajou, puma, tarantula, tree frog, moth, tapir, cockroach, iguana, jaguar, cougar, deer, lemur, orangutan, marmoset, pink dolphin, wild dog, wolf, raccoon, otter, ocelot, three-toed sloth, mosquito, bot fly, bat, and termite.

One-third of the world's birds reside in the Amazon rainforest, including the macaw, parrot, toucan, harpy eagle, crow, ant bird, and umbrella bird. Approximately one-fifth of all freshwater fish are found in the Amazon Basin. Unfortunately, a number of unscrupulous individuals have engaged in illegal wildlife trading, decreasing the number of animals found within the rainforest and further threatening the natural balance of life there.

PEOPLE

Gonzalo and Francisco de Orellana, two Spanish explorers, discovered the Amazon River region in 1541 while looking for valuable minerals and spices. They encountered native people, including a band of women warriors who became known as Amazons. Many of the native people died from diseases brought by explorers to the

New World or from being enslaved. Whole tribes were wiped out. In the 16th century, over 10 million natives resided in the Amazon Rainforest. That number had decreased to less than 200,000 by the beginning of the 21st century.

In Brazil, for example, only 10 percent of the original tribes remain. Some of the poorer members of the tribes that inhabit the Amazon Rainforest today survive on subsistence farming, further destroying valuable resources. Natives within the rainforest eat cassava, yucca, fruits, nuts, fish, insects, and animals such as rabbits, deer, and wild pigs that they shoot with rifles or blowguns. Some tribes, such as the Kayapo, have become more Westernized, enjoying bank and money market accounts, airplanes, tractors, bulldozers, and other luxuries of modern life.

RAINFOREST DESTRUCTION

James Alcock, a professor at Pennsylvania State University, has estimated that at the current rate of destruction, the point of no return in the Amazon Rainforest could be reached as early as 2021. Unchecked destruction could entirely wipe out the rainforest by the middle of the 21st century. Poverty, population growth, greed, and shortsightedness have historically been the major threats to the Amazon forests. Construction, which often operates on the principle of "slash and burn," has posed a serious threat since the middle of the 20th century. Much of the Amazon Rainforest was destroyed by Joao Baptista Figueiredo, the president of Brazil who built the Trans-Amazonian Highway, destroying vast tracts of the forest in western Brazil This highway provided a means for loggers, ranchers, builders, prospectors, and a variety of other people and businesses from around the world to flock to the rainforests, speeding up its destruction. Fire has also become a major threat in recent years as the rainforest has become drier. The fragile lands of the rainforest are also being used for cattle grazing and subsistence farming. The worst period of destruction in the rainforest came between 1978 and 1990 before the destruction of the rainforest became widely known.

Francisco Alves "Chico" Mendes Filho, a Brazilian rubber tapper, union organizer, and ecologist, became the voice of those who were determined to educate the world about the Amazon Rainforest. Mendes was instrumental in the foundation of the National Counsel of the Seringueiros and helped to plan the extraction reserves, which created government-owned conservation areas designed to give rainforest natives control over the production and protection of the Amazon

Rainforest. Mendes was murdered on December 22, 1988, in the doorway of his home. Through the efforts of the Chico Mendes Committee, Darly and Darcy Alves de Silva were charged with his murder. Mendes's death galvanized the conservationists and enhanced their efforts to protect the rainforest.

Some scientists believe that as much as 30 acres of rainforest are being destroyed every minute in the rainforests of the world. As acre after acre of rainforest is being destroyed, nature's natural shield is disappearing, since there are fewer trees to use the carbon dioxide as food through a process called photosynthesis. As a result, levels of carbon dioxide in the atmosphere are increasing every year.

Intrusions into the rainforests have also destroyed valuable resources such as medicinal plants, quinine, muscle relaxers, steroids, and various cancer-fighting drugs.

Seventy percent of the 3,000 drugs with cancerfighting properties that have been identified by the U.S. Cancer Institute are found in the Amazon Rainforest. American drug companies are so convinced of the potential for finding further disease-fighting drugs in the rainforest that some 100 companies have funded projects to study the plants used by native inhabitants of the rainforest for thousands of years.

One third of the Amazon Rainforest is located in Brazil, where authorities believe that as much as 80 percent of all logging done in the rainforest is done illegally. In 2003, authorities launched a satellite system designed to prevent illegal logging in the rainforest. Brazil has also begun to levy fines against multinational corporations that engage in illegal logging.

Peru has been losing approximately 716,000 acres (289,755 hectares) of rainforest a year. In March 1992, the non-profit Amazon

Centre for Environmental Education and Research Foundation (ACEER) opened the Amazon Biosphere Preserve in Peru to increase knowledge of the Peruvian rainforest and to provide protection for this fragile resource. One way that ACEER has done this is through the erection of a canopy walkway project that allows greater access for scientists to study the living matter that resides in the rainforest. The walkway also provides tourists with a firsthand look at the mysteries of the Peruvian rainforest. ACEER's facilities include also bird and butterfly preserves.

Ecuador has been much more remiss than either Brazil or Peru in protecting its section of the Amazon Rainforest. Ecuadorian authorities have permitted logging, road construction, and oil exploration to destroy approximately 466,800 acres (188,907 hectares) of rainforest a year. In February 2001, officials in Ecuador contracted with an international consortium to construct the Oleoducto de Crudos Pesados (Heavy Crude Pipeline) intended to transport crude oil from the rainforest to the Pacific Coast, destroying forests and wildlife and displacing native inhabitants. As a result, only 1 percent of Ecuador's rainforest has survived.

The rainforest in Colombia is host to over 1,815 species of birds, 590 species of amphibians, and 3,200 species of fish. Like Ecuador, Colombia has done little to check the problems caused by illegal logging, mining, pollution, agriculture, and illegal animal piracy. Similarly, Bolivia has done little to stop multinational logging companies and cocoa and soybean farmers from destroying much of its section of the Amazon Rainforest.

Venezuela has had the additional problem of dealing with oil exploration within its region of the rainforest. Big oil companies destroyed much of Venezuela's forests before 1974, when authorities nationalized the oil industry. Belatedly, the Venezuelan government created a number of national parks and passed protective legislation and recognized the rights of native inhabitants of the rainforest.

The Amazon in context

Tropical rainforests are often considered to be the "cradles of biodiversity." Though they cover only about 6% of the Earth's land surface, they are home to over 50% of global biodiversity. Rain forests also take in massive amounts of carbon dioxide and release oxygen through photosynthesis, which has also given them the nickname "lungs of the planet." They also store very large amounts of carbon, and so cutting and burning their biomass contributes to global climate change. Many modern medicines are derived from rainforest plants, and several very important food crops originated in the rainforest, including bananas, mangos, chocolate, coffee, and sugar cane.

In order to qualify as a tropical rainforest, an area must receive over 250 centimeters of rainfall each year and have an average temperature above 24 degrees centigrade, as well as never experiencing frosts. The Amazon rainforest in South America is the largest in the world. The second largest is the Congo in central Africa, and other important rainforests can be found in Central America, the Caribbean, and Southeast Asia. Brazil contains about 40% of the world's remaining tropical rainforest. Its rainforest covers an area of land about 2/3 the size of the continental United States.

There are countless reasons, both anthropocentric and ecocentric, to value rainforests. But they are one of the most threatened types of ecosystems in the world today. It's somewhat difficult to estimate how quickly rainforests are being cut down, but estimates range from between 50,000 and 170,000 square kilometers per year. Even the most conservative estimates project that if we keep cutting rainforests as we are today, within about 100 years there will be none left.

How does a rainforest work?

Rainforests are incredibly complex ecosystems, but understanding a few basics about their ecology will help us understand why clear-cutting and fragmentation are such destructive activities for rainforest biodiversity.

High biodiversity in tropical rainforests means that the interrelationships between organisms are very complex. A single tree may house more than 40 different ant species, each of which has a different ecological function and may alter the habitat in distinct and important ways. Ecologists debate about whether systems that have high biodiversity are stable and resilient, like a spider web composed of many strong individual strands, or fragile, like a house of cards. Both metaphors are likely appropriate in some cases. One thing we can be certain of is that it is very difficult in a rainforest system, as in most others, to affect just one type of organism. Also, clear cutting one small area may damage hundreds or thousands of established species interactions that reach beyond the cleared area.

Pollination is a challenge for rainforest trees because there are so many different species, unlike forests in the temperate regions that are often dominated by less than a dozen tree species. One solution is for individual trees to grow close together, making pollination simpler, but this can make that species vulnerable to extinction if the one area where it lives is clear cut. Another strategy is to develop a mutualistic relationship with a long-distance pollinator, like a specific bee or hummingbird species. These pollinators develop mental maps of where each tree of a particular species is located and then travel between them on a sort of "trap-line" that allows trees to pollinate each other. One problem is that if a forest is fragmented then these trap-line connections can be disrupted, and so trees can fail to be pollinated and reproduce even if they haven't been cut.

The quality of rainforest soils is perhaps the most surprising aspect of their ecology. We might expect a lush rainforest to grow from incredibly rich, fertile soils, but actually, the opposite is true. While some rainforest soils that are derived from volcanic ash or from river deposits can be quite fertile, generally rainforest soils are very poor in nutrients and organic matter. Rainforests hold most of their nutrients in their live vegetation, not in the soil. Their soils do not maintain nutrients very well either, which means that existing nutrients quickly "leech" out, being carried away by water as it percolates through the soil. Also, soils in rainforests tend to be acidic, which means that it's difficult for plants to access even the few existing nutrients. The section on slash and burn agriculture in the previous module describes some of the challenges that farmers face when they attempt to grow crops on tropical rainforest soils, but perhaps the most important lesson is that once a rainforest is cut down and cleared away, very little fertility is left to help a forest regrow.

What is driving deforestation in the Amazon?

Many factors contribute to tropical deforestation, but consider this typical set of circumstances and processes that result in rapid and unsustainable rates of deforestation. This story fits well with the historical experience of Brazil and other countries with territory in the Amazon Basin.

Population growth and poverty encourage poor farmers to clear new areas of rainforest, and their efforts are further exacerbated by government policies that permit landless peasants to establish legal title to land that they have cleared.

At the same time, international lending institutions like the World Bank provide money to the national government for large-scale projects like mining, construction of dams, new roads, and other infrastructure that directly reduces the forest or makes it easier for farmers to access new areas to clear.

The activities most often encouraging new road development are timber harvesting and mining. Loggers cut out the best timber for domestic use or export, and in the process knock over many other less valuable trees. Those trees are eventually cleared and used for wood pulp, or burned, and the area is converted into cattle pastures. After a few years, the vegetation is sufficiently degraded to make it not profitable to raise cattle, and the land is sold to poor farmers seeking out a subsistence living.

Regardless of how poor farmers get their land, they often are only able to gain a few years of decent crop yields before the poor quality of the soil overwhelms their efforts, and then they are forced to move on to another plot of land. Small-scale farmers also hunt for meat in the remaining fragmented forest areas, which reduces the biodiversity in those areas as well.

Another important factor not mentioned in the scenario above is the clearing of rainforest for industrial agriculture plantations of bananas, pineapples, and sugar cane. These crops are primarily grown for export, and so an additional driver to consider is consumer demand for these crops in countries like the United States.

These cycles of land use, which are driven by poverty and population growth as well as government policies, have led to the rapid loss of tropical rainforests. What is lost in many cases is not simply biodiversity, but also valuable renewable resources that could sustain many generations of humans to come. Efforts to protect rainforests and other areas of high biodiversity is the topic of the next section.

How the Amazon Controls the Earth's Climate

A Critical Rain Generator for the Planet

Scientists and environmentalists have proclaimed the accolades of the Amazon rainforest since scientific exploration first began over a hundred years ago, reflecting the region's unique status on the planet. This unique ecosystem contains the world's largest rainforest and spans some 40% of South America, including parts of Brazil, Bolivia, Peru, Ecuador, Colombia, Venezuela, Guyana, and Suriname.

Containing 20% of the world's flowing fresh water, the Amazon River is the world's largest in terms of discharge — eleven times the volume of the Mississippi — draining an area equivalent in size to the United States.

The Amazon rainforest covers only 4% of Earth's surface, yet it is one of the most biodiverse regions on the planet — containing a third of all known terrestrial plant, animal, and insect species. These living organisms are not only inherently valuable simply by adding so much beauty and diversity of life to our world, but they also possess value for humans in the form of food and medicine.

With more than 30 million people living in the Amazon region – 1.6 million of these being indigenous – it is also a hotbed of cultural diversity. More than 400 different indigenous groups call this region home; some are isolated tribes who choose to avoid contact with the outside world.

Covering 6.9 million square kilometers, and containing 10% of all biomass on Earth, the Amazon rainforest also acts as a giant sponge, absorbing and storing massive amounts of carbon dioxide, while emitting 20% of the Earth's oxygen. Many scientists point out that because the forest sequesters carbon dioxide while producing oxygen on such a grand scale, it "plays a critical role in the global carbon cycle that helps to shape the world's climate," leading scientists to dub the Amazon as 'the lungs of the world.'

A new theory suggests that the value of the rainforest is still being understated. The latest research proposes that the Amazon is also the beating 'heart of the Earth,' as millions of trees work together as a kind of 'biotic pump' that releases water vapor into the air. This process creates 'flying rivers' in the atmosphere that circulate water and weather patterns around the globe.

The Heart of the Earth

Originally conceived in 2007 by Russian scientists Anastassia Makarieva and Victor Gorshkov, of the St. Petersburg Nuclear Physics Institute, the biotic pump theory questions the long-standing assumption that rainforests are a consequence of heavy rainfall. The theory contends that instead, some forested regions actually create the conditions necessary that lead to heavy rainfall. Makarieva and Gorshkov assert and claim to have proved that it is "condensation from natural forests" and "not temperature differences, that drive the winds which bring precipitation over land," a mechanism in which the rainforest itself creates its own rainfall, bringing moisture to all terrestrial life.

The process has many stages, beginning with the rainforest drawing water from the ground and releasing the moisture into the atmosphere through the biological process called 'transpiration.'

> *The Amazon rain forest draws water from the ground and releases the moisture into the atmosphere through a process called transpiration.*

Transpiration is evaporation, but it is evaporation of water that has gone through the trees. Think of it like blood in our veins — but unlike blood, the tree water is then pushed up into the sky as a kind of water vapor. – NPR, The Amazon Rainforest is the Lungs of the Planet

One of the leading climate scientists in Brazil focusing on the biotic pump theory is Dr. Antonio Nobre. Much of his research is on how deforestation of the Amazon rainforest affects global weather patterns, climate, and ultimately, the process of transpiration. In an interview with National Public Radio's international correspondent Lulu Garcia-Navarro, Nobre explains how the collective efforts of the millions of trees in the rainforest irrigate the atmosphere, creating massive, invisible flying rivers.

As he illustrates, trees are like geysers acting as conduits that pump water vapor up into the sky. "Transpiration is evaporation, but it's evaporation of water that went through the tree," he says, "so this huge flow of vapour into the atmosphere is like an irrigation [system] upside down." That creates these immense, invisible flying rivers. "Rivers of rainfall," Nobre says. He points out that a calculation for the entire Amazon was done. "20 billion tons of water evaporate per day" in the region. To put that number into perspective, it is more water than what the Amazon River discharges into the Atlantic ocean in one day.

Flying Rivers of the Amazon

Forest transpiration is only the first stage of the biotic pump cycle. As Dr. Nobre points out, the model also shows that forests create ocean-to-land winds that pump the moisture laden currents like airborne rivers across the continents. How can forests create these winds?

In 2015, climate change educator, activist, and founding editor of the environmental newsletter The Ecologist, Peter Bunyard, joined Anastassia Makarieva and Victor Gorshkov on an expedition in the Colombian Amazon aiming to prove the biotic pump theory. Accounting his experience in his article, , the scientist explains that as the large amounts of water vapor transpired by rainforests condenses, it lowers area air pressure. Because air flows from places of high pressure to those of low pressure, this decrease in pressure pulls additional dense air in, and so forests draw in moist air from elsewhere (for example, from over the Atlantic Ocean).

This creates a positive feedback loop that "[generates] an implosion of sufficient strength as to suck up air from the surface. That upwards-directed flow...leads to air moving horizontally over the surface to fill the partial vacuum... Hence the idea that the trade winds—skimming over the surface of the Atlantic Ocean on their way from Africa to equatorial South America—are sucked in as a result of cloud formation over the Amazon's rainforests."

Consequently, as affirmed by the biotic pump theory, the flying rivers of the Amazon carry rainwater in fast moving streams around the Americas. Forests, rather than the ocean, become the low-pressure zone where the moist winds converge to. Moisture sucked in from the east, over the Atlantic, merges with the air vapor transpired by the rainforest and continue to travel west, until the current is eventually blocked by the Andes. At this point, the rivers turn south where they continue to release their moisture in the form of rainfall as far as Argentina. There are even some reports indicating that these systems influence rainfall as far away as the Western United States and Central America.

Life on Earth Without the Amazon

Bunyard is quick to assert the gravity of the situation, insisting the biotic pump theory needs to be accepted by the larger scientific and climatological community before it's too late. Most climatologists agree that continued deforestation will lead to a marked decrease in forest transpiration, and therefore rainfall. However, the general belief is that moisture would still be circulated and generated by oceans and the winds they produce.

Bunyard argues that "those models do not include the biotic pump theory of convection and therefore could possibly be dangerously deficient in their analytical predictions of the impacts both of global warming and in particular of deforestation." He warns that "were the forest to disappear, then according to the theory, moisture would no longer be sucked in and given the natural fall-out rate of rainfall[...]the land would dry out and in all likelihood turn to desert. Were that the case it would be a disaster of momentous proportions, not just dwarfing the likely changes resulting from global warming but indeed compounding them."

If correct, the theory would explain how the deep interiors of forested continents get as much rain as the coast, and how most of Australia turned from forest to desert. It suggests that much of North America could become desert—even without global warming. The idea makes it even more vital that we recognize the crucial role forests play in the well-being of the planet. — New Scientist: Rainforests May Pump Winds Worldwide

The effects that deforestation of the Amazon is having on rainfall and climate are clearly illustrated in neighboring areas — the densely populated central and southern reaches of Brazil — where unprecedented drought has been plaguing the land over the last two years. Calling it "the worst drought in Brazil's history," The Guardian reported that in 2015, more than four million people in urban and suburban areas throughout the country have been affected by water rationing and rolling power cuts."

Protesters in dry neighborhoods have taken to the streets, coffee crops have been hit, and businesses forced to close[…] At least six cities have been hit by blackouts due to weak hydroelectricity generation and high demand for air conditioning as temperatures soar over 35 °C. In response, utilities are burning more fossil fuels, adding to the cost of energy and greenhouse gas emissions." The implications of the report are ominous: drought creates a vicious circle that leads to worsening climate change, that if not addressed and rectified quickly, seem to point towards societal collapse.

The importance of the Amazon rainforest in regulating not only South America's climate but also that of the entire world cannot be overestimated. Like the Earth's cryosphere, the Amazon and other rainforests are essential geographic features of the planet that help regulate the climate and provide habitat for unique wildlife. As with the melting polar regions, the loss of the Amazon to capitalist "resource development" will prove to be a self-destructive act for all of mankind. – Forests Precede Us, Deserts Follow

While some climatologists agree that this disaster is the result of a complex relationship of factors, that include global warming and the unchecked growth of cities, they insist that the disruption of Brazil's weather patterns by the loss of Amazon rainforest is also a contributing factor — and Brazil is not the only country expected to suffer the climatic consequences of this deforestation.

One Princeton study suggested that Amazon deforestation could potentially strengthen patterns of extreme drought in places as far away as California, while other research indicated that recent droughts in Texas and New Mexico might be linked to tree cutting in the Amazon.

Despite the controversy over the biotic pump theory, it is apparent, as evidenced by these numerous studies, that changing the water cycle in the Amazon would have global consequences, not only for human beings but for all life on Earth.

Changing the Dream

As more parts of the world begin to suffer drought and climate change from a variety of destructive global practices and policies, a tipping point is rapidly approaching where dangerous trends will become irreversible.

We are caught in a period of 'technological entrancement' where the worldview of the Global North has become dysfunctional and destructive, creating a radical separation between the human world and the natural world. The dream of the West must be transformed.

There is a different dream that is emerging, a worldview that acknowledges the interconnectedness of all living things, where often, one of the most important roles a human being has is to act as caretaker of the environment and protector of the natural systems that give us life.

Waking up from the trance of separateness creates powerful new possibilities for the future. It is in this spirit of hope that we can come together to nurture a different dream for the world, one that, "brings forth an environmentally sustainable, spiritually fulfilling socially just human presence on this planet."

The Amazon and the politics of greed

There is only one thing that drives Brazilian President Jair Bolsonaro and that is profits.

He is the worst kind of capitalist, reminiscent of the cowboys of a long gone era who thought it was justifiable to destroy indigenous communities by killing or assimilating their inhabitants, who had no conscience whatsoever when it came to destroying critical natural vegetation to make way for slash and burn development.

This is nothing but a colonial mentality borne from greed and self-interest.

When Bolsonaro was a lawmaker in the 1990s he had articulated how he had admired the ruthlessness with which the American cavalry had fought Native Americans during the expansion of the US.

"The North American Cavalry were the competent ones because they decimated indigenous people in the past and today

they don't have a problem in their country."

Bolsonaro made it no secret in the weeks before he was elected president that he planned to give people guns in order to move the indigenous people off their land, and advocated the destruction of the indigenous reservations.

The reservation of land for the indigenous population is seen by the inhabitants as the only way to safeguard their way of living, language and culture.

But to Bolsonaro indigenous reservations are "anachronistic," a sentiment ridden with racism and superiority. "Indigenous people don't lobby, speak our language, and yet today they manage to have 14% of our national territory...one of their intentions is to hold us back," Bolsonaro is quoted as having said.

Bolsonaro's other infamous statements include calling indigenous people parasites, and advocating discriminatory eugenically devised forms of birth control.

This squares with his other outrageously racist statements about Afro-Brazilians being obese and lazy and living off the rest of society, saying "I don't think they're even good for procreation anymore."

Bolsonaro has also depicted people from Haiti, Africa and the Middle East as the "scum of humanity," saying the army should take care of them.

Sadly the Brazilian people were well aware of Bolsonaro's extreme racism when they elected him, just as much as they were aware of his intention to destroy large parts of the Amazon rainforest to make way for capitalist development - whether in the form of mining, logging or agri-business.

The new Brazilian Congress under Bolsonaro's leadership wasted no time in approving reforms that would allow industrial agriculture on indigenous reserves.

Bolsonaro's promises to open up the Amazon to capitalist development was also fast tracked, and in his first six months in office deforestation peaked.

Indigenous tribes turned to the courts to protect them, and after they won cases to stop oil exploration, weeks later the protagonists started fires to burn the natural environment, leaving devastation in their wake.

The reason why the Amazon has been engulfed in flames recently is largely due to the sense of impunity created by Bolsonaro that there will be no consequences when big business takes matters into their own hands.

It is now common knowledge that the record number of fires in the Amazon has coincided with a significant drop in fines for environmental violations, with the lowest number of fines having been issued in a decade.

The number of fines over the past seven months have dropped by a third, and the number of fires burning has increased by 84%. Bolsonaro infamously said, "fines for environmental crimes is an industry that needs to be abolished."

Bolsonaro had always warned that he would weaken the influence of Brazil's Environmental Protection Agency Ibama, and true to his word, the actions of Ibama have decreased by 20% during the first six months of the year, compared to the same period last year.

Hundreds of government workers who are supposed to enforce Brazil's environmental laws have now signed an open letter saying that Brazil's environmental protection system could collapse if nothing changes.

Ibama has been suffering budget cuts, staff reductions in remote areas, political interference, and a weakening of environmental regulations.

In June and July Ibama was unable to carry out its operations in the state of Para where deforestation has been soaring, primarily because the police have refused to provide back up.

According to the law, Ibama agents are legally allowed to destroy equipment found in protected areas that would be used for deforestation. But now the agents are afraid to burn such equipment as Bolsonaro has come out saying that nobody should be burning machines.

In the midst of the raging fires over a week ago, Bolsonaro made a speech in which he reinforced his plans to "bring economic dynamism to the Amazon."

In a situation where a belligerent leader is determined to pursue policies detrimental to one of the most bio-diverse regions of the globe, there does need to be a robust reaction on the part of the international community, and there certainly should be repercussions.

At least Finland has been vocal and called for the EU to ban Brazilian beef imports in protest against the decimation that Bolsonaro is leaving in his wake. France and Ireland have also said that they will not ratify the trade deal with South America that took years to negotiate.

VF Corporation, a major buyer of Brazilian leather, has warned that it might cancel leather purchases over concerns about the relationship between *agribusiness and the fires that have devastated the Amazon rainforest.*

VF Corporation supplies Brazilian leather to Timberland, North Face, Eagle Creek, Dickies, Vans and Kipling.

Brazil's leather goods organisation wrote to the Brazilian Minister of Environment to inform them about the warning, adding to growing concern among business leaders in Brazil that the government needs to contain the damage done to the country's image.

This is the type of pushback that we need to see emanating from the private sector as global outrage soars.

But there also needs to be more cognizance in the international community of the other factors that have driven the desire on the part of Brazil's right wing government to surge ahead with the clearing of land in the Amazon for profit.

The ongoing trade war between the US and China has played a significant role in that China has stopped buying US soybeans as a retaliatory measure to the US hiking tariffs on Chinese goods.

China has turned to Brazil as a source of soybeans, which has seen exports surge, and fuelled Brazil's ecological disaster. Brazil went from exporting soybeans to China for half a year, to selling them year round, providing an additional 30-40 million tons of the crop.

From May last year to April this year China imported 71 million tons of soybeans from Brazil, which is equal to the amount of all Chinese soybean exports five years ago.

The result has been farmers setting fire to more and more land to make way for crops due to China's hunger for soybeans, while American farmers have put their crops in storage.

For Bolsonaro "environmental issues matter only to vegans who eat vegetables," and thus ecological reserves hinder the forward march of capitalism. To Brazil's leader there needs to be fewer national parks, less rainforest, and more development.

Just as our northern brothers in Europe have spoken out against such madness, it is time for South Africa to do the same. It may even have more weight coming from a BRICS partner.

Capitalism and greed ignited the Amazon rainforest fires

Fires are plaguing the Amazon rainforest, which is home to a vast range of biodiversity, indigenous tribes and botanical wonders that actively reduce greenhouse gas emissions.

Many are pulling out their wallets to protect this important entity with donations, and taking to social media to send their thoughts and prayers to the Amazon. Donations are incredibly important to fight back against the greed that goes hand-in-hand with agribusiness groups such as the largest caucus within Brazil's congress, the ruralista bloc.

However, many are too optimistic about the impact of their donations and fail to acknowledge how complex the subject matter is.

Because the climate is at a catastrophic state, the Amazon rainforest is a crucial environmental body that must stay protected.

Although the Amazon rainforest spans across nine countries, Brazil has been at the forefront of the conversation in regards to deforestation within the Amazon. Under the rule of Brazil's President Jair Bolsonaro, deforestation has risen 88% in June, compared to the previous year.

Several countries have joined The Paris Climate Agreement to prevent the global temperature from rising 2 degrees Celsius, which mainstream scientists have deemed the point of "no return" for climate change. Unfortunately, Bolsonaro has moved Brazil in the opposite direction of this agreement.

During his campaign, Bolsonaro ran on platforms which advocated for the extension of a highway through the rainforest and power plants within it. Furthermore, Bolsonaro promised to reduce environmental protections, and reallocate the land and resources that have been promised to indigenous tribes of the Amazon rainforest.

When a leader eliminates the post of secretary on climate change and strips the environment ministry of all authority, which Bolsonaro has done, it is clear that protecting the environment is not in their interest.

Due to the greedy nature of capitalism, many see the Amazon rainforest as an entity, which needs to be disregarded for the sake of economic advancement.

Allowing individual agribusiness owners to continuously expand, puts the Earth and all its inhabitants in a precarious and unsafe position. If humans, including Bolsonaro, want to continue living in a secure environment, delicate ecosystems such as the Amazon rainforest must not be seen as a roadblock to one's livelihood.

The exploitation of Mother Nature in the name of economic advancement is just lazy.

By adhering to historic trends of industrialization while putting the environment at risk, one is following the same cycle of destruction, while refusing to think outside of the box.

Maybe they're just dull, or maybe they don't care, but when a person in power such as Bolsonaro rejects the modern reality of our environment, they are proving that they are both unaware and foolish.

In a world where the effects of climate change are becoming undisguised, biological entities that actively reduce the amount of greenhouse gas emissions are needed now more than ever.

Yes, Brazil deserves the chance to advance economically, but they need to consider advancement that doesn't follow an outdated context of industrialization.

Bolsonaro needs to approach this situation with more creativity. Prosperity doesn't need to put the Earth and its lungs at stake. Focusing on more than just the industry of agribusiness, opens the door to a safer form of economic advancement.

Perhaps creating a reward system for individual agribusiness owners who make active steps toward practicing environmentally-safe standards for their business could be implemented by the Brazilian government. It would work to combat land degradation and deforestation.

Regardless of how it's done, the interests of the agribusiness industry needs to be put on the backburner, before the whole world is ablaze.

While most are watching the terrors of the Amazon fires engulf into a deeper depression in relation to climate change, direct focus needs to be made to combat the evils of deforestation on a local level.

Getting involved with reforestation projects such as the One Tree Planted organization, is a clear way to take action.

Rather than mourning what is already lost, each individual can get involved by creating their own oasis for environmental protection.

Nature-based solutions, such as reforestation, will be discussed at the United Nations General Assembly occurring this year, and every individual must raise their voices to address how important reforestation is in our modern environment, where greedy capitalists are putting their needs before the betterment of the planet.

A strict ban on deforestation must be implemented, and those that do not adhere to it must know the severity of their selfishness.

Europe can help save the Amazon by changing itself

Europe did not light the fires ravaging the Amazon, but it did provide some of the matches.

There is plenty the EU can do to save and protect the Amazon rainforest - and much of that begins at home.

The infernos still tearing their way through large swathes of the Amazon are transforming the most fertile and biologically diverse land in the world into a charred, desolate landscape.

In the first eight months of this year, the total number of fires increased by 82 percent compared with last year. In August, a group of farmers in Para state had, in a show of solidarity with Brazil's President Jair Bolsonaro, reportedly declared a "day of fire". A total of 26,000 fires were recorded that month.

Mercosur

The blame for the fires has been squarely placed on the shoulders of Brazil's new far-right president, who is a conspiracy theorist and climate change denier, notoriously pro-agribusiness and ranchers, and rabidly opposed to the indigenous peoples of the rainforest.

However, the rest of the world cannot absolve itself of responsibility that easily. While Bolsonaro is responsible for the accelerated devastation of the Amazon, the rainforest has been under attack for decades.

Since 1970, nearly 800,000 km² of Amazonian rainforest has been cleared, which is an area larger than France and about the same size as Turkey. Although forest loss to date has been due to human activity, scientists fear we may soon reach a tipping point when tree loss starts to feed on itself, destroying much of the ecosystem.

The vast majority of the deforestation in Brazil and other Amazon states has been due to the clearing of land for cattle rearing to feed the world's voracious appetite for beef and leather.

For its part, the EU imports 120,000 tonnes a year of Brazilian beef, and this figure would balloon under a free trade deal recently agreed with the Mercosur bloc (Brazil, Argentina, Paraguay and Uruguay).

Sustainable

Another major cause of deforestation in the Amazon is soy production, which is intensifying in light of the current US-Sino trade war. Although China is the world's largest importer of soybeans, the EU is the world's premier importer of soymeal and the second largest importer of soybeans.

"These vast flows of animal feedstocks (soybeans and soymeal) being imported into the EU have significant implications for land use in exporting countries, principally in South

America, as vast tracts of land are given over to soy monocultures," the report explains.

"The area planted with soybeans in South America is continuously growing with the combined soybean area of Brazil, Argentina, Paraguay and Bolivia expanding two-and-half times between 1988 and 2008, from 17 million hectares to 42 million hectares."

"Ironically, despite Europe's significant contribution to deforestation in the Amazon and other forested areas, this is not counted when the EU is measuring its sustainability," notes Patrizia Heidegger, director for global policies and sustainability at the EEB.

"This enables us to ignore our footprint in the outside world, look at the growing forest cover in Europe and believe we are becoming more sustainable."

Flames

Unless something dramatic changes, this spells devastation for the Amazon and other rainforests around the world, including the unique flora and fauna they host, not to mention the indigenous peoples who live there and act as custodians of these forests.

The European Union can save the Amazon, and other rainforests, by halting the import of goods produced on land that was formerly forest. An alliance of 26 leading NGOs has urged the EU to pass legislation that will guarantee that all products sold in Europe are free from deforestation and human rights abuses.

"The EU is in a rare position to act for the Amazon by using its unique market leverage," said Hannah Mowat, campaigns coordinator at Fern, a Brussels-based organisation dedicated to protecting forests and the rights of people depending on them, which is a member of the EEB network.

"Forget the unaccepted €20 million offer from the G7, let's talk about the €6 billion euro leverage we have, which is what the EU spends on importing rainforest-destroying products like soy or beef," insists Nick Meynen, policy officer for environmental and economic justice at the EEB.

"Rather than ratifying the EU-Mercosur trade deal that would fan the flames only further, erect new trade tariffs based on the carbon emissions associated with the import of products such as soy, leather or beef."

Evolve

Another option would be to divert the equivalent of some or all of these funds to finance the restoration and preservation of the rainforest.

"Beyond Mercosur, all trade deals between EU and the outside world must include safeguards

to protect biodiversity and contribute to our climate targets," says Célia Nyssens, agriculture policy officer at the EEB.

Renegotiating harmful trade deals is not enough. We also need to tackle damaging lifestyles.

Margarita Mediavilla is professor of system dynamics and senior scientist with LOCOMOTION, an EU-backed project which is modelling scenarios for the transition towards a carbon-neutral and sustainable future.

She observes: "As long as our dietary patterns continue to evolve towards more meat products, the pressure to gain land from rainforests worldwide will increase."

Transition

"There is no way around the fact that we have to reduce our consumption of animal products," insist Nyssens. *"We need to transform the way we produce and consume meat and dairy."*

The only way to reduce our pressure on rainforests is to phase out industrial livestock farming, which relies on imported protein crops like soya to feed animals.

This will inevitably lead to lower livestock numbers in Europe. In order to reduce the pressure on land resources so as to protect forests and natural ecosystems, people need to eat fewer animal proteins and more plant proteins.

"The LOCOMOTION model will include the global picture of land competition among uses: energy, food, urban, natural spaces and forests," explains Mediavilla. *"This module will enable us to explore how dietary changes would influence climate change mitigation."*

Many will regard such lifestyle changes as sacrifices, but reducing meat consumption will actually improve our health and wellbeing. In addition, well-managed pastures can help us achieve our climate and biodiversity objectives, explains Nyssens.

"The key is to help our farmers transition to this new system through government support and consumer choices," she adds.

The U.N. Could Save the Amazon With One Simple Move

The Amazon is burning. Nearly 75,000 fires have started in the iconic Brazilian rainforest this

year to date, an 84 percent increase from the year before. Since August 10, a spate of intentionally set fires have been raging in the Amazon. But Brazil's president Jair Bolsonaro, who took office in January, let them burn for two weeks before sending firefighters to put them out following an international outcry.

Fires ravaging the Amazon pose imminent peril to the 34 million people and 3 million species of animals and plants that live in the world's largest rainforest, which covers 2 million square miles.

Damage from the raging fires will change the face of the planet. The rainforest is home to 10 percent of the species on Earth, including many types of plants and animals that cannot be found anywhere else.

"The loss of the Amazon's biodiversity will be beyond devastating for the planet," Dahr Jamail wrote in Truthout, noting that many scientists consider the Amazon to be the Earth's most important site of biodiversity.

'An International Crisis'

French president Emmanuel Macron tweeted, "Our house is burning. Literally," and exhorted, "Members of the G7 Summit, let's discuss this emergency first order in two days!" Bristling at Macron's exhortation, Bolsonaro wrote on Twitter, "The French president's suggestion that Amazon issues be discussed at the G-7 without participation by the countries in the region evokes a colonialist mentality that is out of place in the 21st century."

In light of Bolsonaro's refusal to provide resources to extinguish the fires, Macron threatened to block the Mercosur-European Union trade deal. Bolsonaro capitulated. He allocated $7 million and sent 44,000 troops and military aircraft to the burning areas.

But that falls short of what is needed to put out the fires and save the Amazon. "We're talking about battling what will be hundreds of fires burning simultaneously, beyond any road network, distributed across thousands of miles," according to Douglas Morton, head of the Biospheric Sciences Laboratory at NASA's Goddard Space Flight Center. "It's quite a challenge to mobilize resources for one of these fires, but to simultaneously track down and put out a number of these sorts of fires ... demands essentially a full press," adding, "You really do need thousands of people."

The countries in the G-7 – the U.S., Britain, France, Germany, Italy, Japan and Canada – donated $20 million to help fight the fires, but Bolsonaro refused to accept the money unless Macron apologizes. Bolsonaro is playing games while the Amazon burns.

Donald Trump, who skipped the climate meeting at the G-7 summit, later said he hadn't agreed to contribute to the $20 million because of lack of coordination with Bolsonaro.

Moreover, even if accepted, this money would not be sufficient. Rick Swan, of the International Association of Fire Fighters, told The Washington Post that, by comparison, to extinguish the 2017 Tubbs Fire in Northern California, "the costs alone were $100 million."

In other words, a massive international effort is needed to end the Amazon fires.

Bolsonaro's Appeal to Anti-Colonial Politics Is Deeply Cynical

Those who are critical of ongoing colonial and neocolonial dynamics but who are not entirely familiar with the context of the fires in Brazil may at first be skittish about backing international efforts to pressure Bolsonaro to end the fires. In truth, however, Bolsonaro's appeal to anti-colonial politics is deeply cynical and should not deter progressives with anti-colonial commitments from backing international endeavors to end the fires.

The cynicism of Bolsonaro's anti-colonial appeal is evident in the context of widespread popular protests in which Brazilians have marched holding signs with messages, such as "The Amazon belongs to the world, and we need the world's help right now" and "SOS." Protesters took part in some 30 demonstrations across Brazil last weekend, and thousands of demonstrators marching in Rio chanted, "The Amazon stays, out with Bolsonaro."

Indigenous peoples in Brazil have also made clear that they hold Bolsonaro's government responsible for the destruction of the Amazon. The Coordination of Indigenous Organizations of the Brazilian Amazon (COIAB) issued a statement expressing "extreme concern about the rapid destruction of the Amazon rainforest, home to our families and to all the resources we need to live." COIAB stated, "The related record rates of deforestation and outbreaks of fire are a consequence of the anti-indigenous and anti-environmental genocidal speeches of this government."

A group of Indigenous Huni Kuin leaders recently called for a stop to the fires, saying: "Nature is crying and we are crying. If we don't stop this destruction of Mother Nature, future generations will live in a completely different world to the one we live in today. This is Mother Nature's cry, asking us to help her. And we are working today so that humanity has a future. But if we don't stop this destruction, we will be the ones that will be extinguished, burned and the sky will descend upon us, which has already begun to happen."

The U.N. Security Council Should Order International Firefighters and Economic Boycott

As empowered by the United Nations Charter, the Security Council should find that the fires in the Amazon pose a "threat to the peace" and order measures to restore and maintain international peace and security. Those measures "may include complete or partial interruption of economic relations."

The Council should require that member states refrain from entering into trade agreements with

Brazil unless and until it agrees to allow international economic and physical firefighting assistance. As Moira Birss, Amazon Watch's finance campaign director said in a release issued by the Institute for Public Accuracy (IPA), "Now that the world is finally paying attention, it's important to also understand that governments and companies around the world are emboldening Bolsonaro's toxic policies when they enter trade agreements with his government or invest in agribusiness companies operating in the Amazon."

In addition, the Council should order member states to contribute money and personnel to fight the fires raging in the Amazon.

There is precedent for this type of resolution. In 1985, the Council passed Resolution 569, which condemned the South African government's policy of apartheid. It urged UN members to adopt measures including suspension of all new investment in South Africa, prohibition of the sale of South African currency and coins, restrictions on cultural relations and sports, suspension of guaranteed export loans, prohibition of new nuclear contracts, and prohibition of sales of computer equipment that could be used by the South African police and army. The international boycott of South Africa led to the end of the apartheid regime.

All UN member countries are bound by the resolutions of the Security Council. Article 25 of the Charter says, "The members of the United Nations agree to accept and carry out the decisions of the Security Council." And Article 49 states that the UN members "shall join in affording mutual assistance in carrying out the measures" upon which the Council decides.

Bolsonaro's Policies Have Exacerbated the Fires

Fires do not ignite themselves in the rainforest. "Basically, the Amazon hadn't burnt in hundreds of thousands or millions of years," said William Magnusson, a biodiversity specialist at the National Institute of Amazonian Research in Brazil. According to National Geographic, "A growing number of manmade fires have plagued the Amazon in recent years, imperiling the ecosystem. The rainforest is not built for fire."

Farmers in the Amazon cut down trees to clear the area for planting. Miners and loggers start fires to cover their illegal activities. And some fires are set to force Indigenous peoples from their land. Bolsonaro, however, has fanned the flames in the Amazon.

A New York Times analysis found that for the first six months of 2019, Bolsonaro's pro-

development, anti-environmental policies led to a 20 percent decrease in enforcement measures aimed at protecting against deforestation, as compared to the same period in 2018.

"Bolsonaro must take immediate, comprehensive steps to not only extinguish these fires but also address the root causes of this environmental catastrophe: the roll-back of environmental and indigenous rights protections and the recklessness of the profit-seeking agribusiness industry," Christian Poirier, program director at Amazon Watch, said on the IPA release. But, he added, "This burden isn't on the Brazilian government alone. We are all global citizens of our shared planet and must take shared responsibility for its preservation."

We must act internationally to save the precious Amazon rainforest. Citizens of the 15 member countries on the Security

Council should pressure their governments to vote in favour of a resolution calling for an economic boycott of Brazil and the provision of resources to quell the forest fires. The future of our planet is at stake.